My Nature Activity Book

Written by Catriona Clarke

Illustrated by Marek Jagucki

RISING ★ STARS

On a nature walk

Let's go for a nature walk.

Are there minibeasts lurking under the logs?

Are there birds nesting in the trees?

What can we do with these materials that we found on the ground?

smooth stones

pine cones

Pine cone hedgehogs

Pine cones come from pine trees. Some of the seeds inside the cones will grow into new pine trees one day.

Make a hedgehog using a pine cone and some soft clay.

(1) Use four pieces of soft clay for the legs and one for the head.

(2) Add googly eyes and a clay nose.

Pebble art

Smooth stones called pebbles come from the beach or near rivers.

1. Paint pebbles or flat stones to look like bees or ladybirds ... or anything you like!

2. When the pebble is dry, cover it with clear varnish to stop the paint chipping.

Tree rubbings

Leaves grow on trees. Some trees grow fruit and blossom too.

leaves

fruit

plum tree

blossom tree

1 Hold a piece of paper against the trunk of a tree.

2 Use a crayon or oil pastel to make a rubbing.

Flower bookmarks

Around the world, flowers bloom in spring and summer.

stem

petals

1. Use an ice-lolly stick to make the stem of your flower bookmark.

2. Cut out shapes from paper or felt for the petals.

3. Glue them onto the stem.

4. Use a button for the middle of your flower.

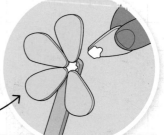

Save the bees

Sometimes bees get tired, but you can help by feeding them.

(1) Mix two spoonfuls of sugar with one spoonful of water.

(2) Put the mixture on a spoon or a small plate outside.

3 Watch from indoors or a safe distance to see if the bee takes a drink.

Cress eggheads

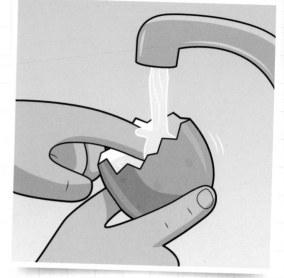

(1) Start with an empty eggshell.

(2) Wash out the shell and leave it to dry.

(3) Put the shell into an eggcup and draw a funny face on it!

4 Place some damp cotton wool inside the shell.

5 Sprinkle one teaspoon of cress seeds on top.

6 Leave the shell on a sunny windowsill for a week. Watch it grow!

Bird snacks

In winter, hungry birds need extra food.

1. Spread honey on the outside of a cardboard tube.

2. Roll the sticky cardboard tube in a tray of bird seed.

3. Make a loop from string at the top of the feeder.

4. Hang your bird feeder outside from a small branch or twig.

branch

birds

feeder

Leaf spotting

To tell which tree is which, look at its leaves.

holly

willow

rowan

How many of these trees can you spot on your next nature walk?

sycamore

horse chestnut

oak

birch

Talk about the book

Answer the questions:

1 Where do pine cones come from?

2 Where are pebbles usually found?

3 Why do you need to use an empty eggshell for the cress egghead activity?

4 Why do the bee and bird feeders have to be placed outside?

5 Which craft project from the book is your favourite and why?

6 What might you find on a nature walk close to your home?